Business Games

A Resource Book of Problems, Issues, and Ethics

Jenny Mawer

ITP
BUSINESS

Language Teaching Publications
35 Church Road, Hove BN3 2BE

© **LTP 1992**
ISBN 0906717 98 1

Photocopying

The Author

Jenny Mawer is a freelance ESP teacher. After graduating in Mathematics from Queen Mary College London she worked both in business and in a Management Training institution before moving into TEFL. She has specialised in Business English Training for more than 10 years working both in UK and outside on company contracts in France, Germany, Spain, Italy and Turkey.

Her special interests in TEFL are promoting confidence, fluency and listening skills which she sees as the fundamental areas of importance for all business people.

Her MA(TEFL) thesis was on the topic of using micro-computers in TEFL.

Acknowledgements

Cover design by Anna Macleod
Design by Hamza Arcan
Photographs courtesy of Zefa
Illustration on page 17 courtesy of Luncheon Vouchers Ltd.
Printed in England by Commercial Colour Press, London E7

To the Teacher

Business Games is a resource book for teachers. It presents activities designed to provide business students with an opportunity to develop fluency.

The topics are business-orientated, but all of them can be used successfully without any job-specific or even business-specific knowledge. They require only an awareness of contemporary life.

Most of the activities require very little preparatory reading which means that they can be set up in the minimum possible time, allowing the maximum time for the activity itself. For the same reason, the activities can be used at all levels from elementary to advanced, providing teachers realise that individual groups or students should be allowed to perform to the level of their own competence. Providing teachers vary their expectations, students from many different backgrounds can be given a feeling of achievement.

Business Problems

These activities are not complex business simulations. The word 'game' conveys many things — teams, co-operation, competitiveness, winning, relaxation and so on. All games involve some of these factors, but few games involve all. So it is with the activities in this book. They are game-like in that they are to be treated as relatively relaxed activities, done in a fixed period of time, involving group and pair co-operation, and there should be some kind of decisive result — usually a decision. The activities will work in class to the extent that the teacher directs a way of proceeding and a time limit, and then the students take the activity seriously on their own terms.

Business Issues and Ethics

The discussion starters in these sections provide short 'bites' which can be used in many different ways:

      — to introduce a topic
      — for 10 minutes at the end of a lesson
      — for group work with a written outcome

The most important feature of these 2 sections is the wealth of ideas, stated simply, to stimulate pair, group, or class discussion.

They are laid out in such a way that, when copied, they can be cut up and a different issue given to each student, pair, or group.

Contents

Business Problems

Business Issues

Business **E**thics

Teachers' **N**otes

1 _____ The Citibus Problem

The Problem

You work for a firm of transport consultants employed by Citibus who operate the city's bus system. You have studied the system and also done a survey of bus users.

The investigations show what the public think:

> **INFOTEC**
>
> TRANSPORT CONSULTANTS
>
> DRAFT REPORT
>
> ON
>
> CITIBUS
>
> SUMMARY OF SURVEY RESULTS
>
> Fares are too high
>
> Bus stops are not conveniently placed
>
> Buses are infrequent
>
> Buses are delayed in traffic jams
>
> Buses are dirty
>
> Some areas are not well-served by buses
>
> Buses finish at midnight
>
> Buses are overcrowded
>
> Timetable information is difficult to get
>
> Occasionally buses break down

In Groups

In groups discuss each problem and decide how it could be solved. Citibus has some money for capital investment but it is limited. You cannot just throw money at the problems.

Action

You will have to report on your ideas to a board meeeting of Citibus.

2 _____ The Cititrain Survey

The Problem

You work for a firm of transport consultants employed by Cititrain who operate the city's surburban train system. You have studied the system and also done a survey of train users.

The investigations show that people think:

1 Trains are overcrowded

2 The carriages are not comfortable

3 Trains are dirty

4 Trains are often late or cancelled

5 Car parking at stations is inadequate

6 Waiting areas are cold in winter

7 Difficult to get timetable information

8 Information telephones are always engaged

9 No information is available on delays

10 Trains are not frequent enough in the rush hour

In Groups

In groups discuss each problem and decide how it could be solved.
Cititrain has some money for capital investment but it is limited. You can not just throw money at the problem.

Action

You will have to report on your ideas to a board meeeting of Cititrain.

3 _____ Company Cars

The Problem

You are the Purchasing Manager for your company.

You are responsible for buying company cars. Within the next few weeks you have to buy cars for the following people:

Elizabeth Sinclair takes important mail between branches within a 20-mile radius. Recently the rapidly increasing costs of this service have been examined by the finance department and you have been instructed to control further increases.

John Shaw is a salesman. He travels long distances each year carrying large quantities of samples. The sales department have also asked you to keep down costs as much as possible.

Henry Baker drives important visitors to and from the station and the factory every day. There is no other company car available for this important service for your visitors.

Philip Lucas is the new Finance Manager. He joined the company to implement the new economy campaign. He frequently finds that he has important discussions with visitors in the car while he is driving to another factory.

In Groups

First discuss the characteristics of a car which would be suitable for each of these employees and fill in the worksheet.

Worksheet

Elizabeth Sinclair

Reliability_____

Noise _____

Seats_____

Luggage Space _____

Running Costs_____

John Shaw

Reliability_____

Noise _____

Seats_____

Luggage Space _____

Running Costs_____

Henry Baker

Reliability_____

Noise _____

Seats_____

Luggage Space _____

Running Costs_____

Philip Lucas

Reliability_____

Noise _____

Seats_____

Luggage Space _____

Running Costs_____

Action

Now you will be given a summary of the relevant characteristics of 6 possible cars. Look carefully at the characteristics of each car.

Then discuss with your group how each car fulfills your list of characteristics and decide which car the group would recommend for each person.

>

Car Information Sheet

The following information is based on surveys published in The Car Buying Guide, published by Which Magazine.

Car	Reliability	Noise	Seats	Luggage space (litres)	Fuel consumption (mpg)	Running cost per week
Vauxhall Cavalier 1.6 Saloon	Average	Engine noise	Comfortable	480/860	34	£26
Renault 21 1.7	Average	Good in the front Noisier in the back	Soft, fairly comfortable	465/675	35	£ 27
Ford Sierra 1.6	A little below average	Not excessive	Comfortable	400/775	31	£27
Honda Accord 1.6	Above average	Quiet	Well-shaped, firm. Limited headroom in the back	445	32	£30
Mazda 626	Better than average	Volume not great	Comfortable, limited legroom in the back	400/880	34	£26
Audi 80 1.8	Much better than average	Good in the front Noisier in the back	Not much head room or legroom in the back	305	31	£32

Notes_____

_____

_____

_____

_____

_____

_____

_____

4   The Best Policy

The Problem

You are the Travel Organiser for your company which has many executives travelling round the world. Because it is cheaper, you want to find a standard business travel insurance policy which will operate for any of your executives when they have a business trip which involves flying.

	Silver Lining Insurance	Executive Insurance	Loss Support Insurance	B.T. Insurance
Premium per flight + daily cost	£1.50 £1.00	£1.50 £1.50	£1.00 £1.25	£2.00 £1.00
Maximum medical benefits	£1m	£500,000	£750,000	no limit
Cover for journey delays	yes	no	yes	yes

Total claimable for loss of:-

	Silver Lining Insurance	Executive Insurance	Loss Support Insurance	B.T. Insurance
***valuables**	£250	£250	£200	£500
***cash**	£200	£400	£200	£300
***personal belongings (clothing etc.)**	£1,000	£1,200	£800	£1,000
***documents**	£200	£250	£200	£200
***equipment** (pc, dictaphone, fax, etc)	£1,500	£2,000	£1,500	£3,000

Action

Discuss and decide which policy to take out.

5 _____ **M**oving **H**ouse

The **P**roblem

Robert Taylor has recently accepted a new job as Production Manager with Empire Chemicals. The headquarters and main factory of Empire Chemicals is located in Southdown, a town in the South of England. At present the Taylor family live in the North of England and so they have to move house.

Empire Chemicals will pay Mr Taylor £27,000 pa. and they will provide him with a company car but they insist that their Production Manager lives no more than 5 miles from the factory.

Mrs Taylor is a nurse. At the moment she works in a local hospital, 10 miles from their present house. She has a small car so that she can travel to and from work.

The Taylors have 3 children - 2 daughters who are 16 and 8 and a son who is 12. The elder daughter is taking her final school exams this year.

Because the Taylor family like to eat fresh fruit and vegetables, they prefer to grow their own. Mr Taylor is keen on DIY.

Mr Taylor's relocation package includes all moving expenses and, in addition, his travel and hotel expenses for 8 weeks.

Their present house will sell for about £55,000 but there is an outstanding mortgage of £30,000. Most building societies will grant a mortgage = 3 x annual salary.

Today is January 31st.

*The Taylors'
old house*

In **G**roups

Read this information, then discuss the family's requirements and fill in the worksheet.

>

Worksheet

First think about the Taylors' house and the things that it must be/have. Consider the price, moving date, the number of rooms, location, etc.

The Taylors' house must:

1. _____
2. _____
3. _____
4. _____
5. _____

Now think about what the Taylors want their house to be/have. Think about the Taylor family and the way they live.

The Taylors want:

1. _____
2. _____
3. _____
4. _____
5. _____
6. _____
7. _____
8. _____
9. _____
10. _____

Action

Next read the information about properties.
Finally choose the house that is most suitable for the Taylor family.
You will be asked to present your choice and give your reasons for choosing it.

>

Southdown Property Services

- **Upper Dean, Southdown.** New detached house available at the end of May/beginning of June. Lounge, dining room, 4 bedrooms (one with en-suite bathroom) all with built-in wardrobes, 2nd bathroom, fully fitted kitchen. Gas central heating. Integral garage. Easily-maintained garden. £105,500

- In **Deanbrook village**, 10 miles from Southdown, a bungalow with 4 bedrooms, bathroom and separate toilet, through lounge/dining room, cloakroom, electric central heating, double garage, well-stocked garden. £103,000

- **Southbrook village**, 5 miles from the centre of Southdown. 25-year old semi-detached house with lounge/dining room, large kitchen, 3 bedrooms, newly renovated bathroom. Large garden with well-kept lawns, flowerbeds and well established vegetable/fruit garden. Separate garage. Convenient for the shops and schools. £110,000

- **Brookpark estate.** Flat, in 3-storey block, with garage, on the edge of the estate. Balcony with a lovely view over the park, large living room, separate dining room, 4 bedrooms, bathroom. Small but well-fitted kitchen with built-in appliances. £104,750

- 2 miles north of the centre of **Southdown**, 5 minutes' walk from the hospital. Large Edwardian house with outbuildings, small, walled town garden. Lounge, dining room, cloaks., study/breakfast room, large kitchen, 5 bedrooms, 2 bathrooms. In need of renovation. £105,000

- Ten-minute bus ride south of the centre of **Southdown**. A small detached house on a large plot. 3 bedrooms, luxury bathroom, lounge, kitchen/dining room. Carport. Well-planned garden. Gas central heating. Shop/post office within 2 minutes' walk. £99,500

- **Lower Dean.** Well-maintained semi-detached house recently re-decorated and extended to give 4 bedrooms, 2 bathrooms, lounge, dining room, study. Average-sized garden, garage. Regular bus service to town centre. £107,500

The **P**roblem

Your company is interested in providing lunch-time eating arrangements for all employees. Your choice is between creating a staff canteen or providing luncheon vouchers which can be exchanged in local restaurants, cafes and some food shops.

In **G**roups

In groups of 3 first create the profile for a company by completing the following **Company Profile**:

1. The size of the company:
      number of managers
      number of office workers
      number of production workers

2. Location:
      in city centre
      away from the city centre
      on a business park/industrial estate
      in the suburbs

3. Description of the site:
      open parkland/fully built-up

4. Other facilities:

5. Transport used by the staff (%):
      car
      public bus
      train
      company-run bus
      bike
      on foot
      other

6. What percentage of employees live within:
      2 mile radius
      10 mile radius
      more than 10 miles

7. Existing lunch hour arrangements:
      fixed lunch hour
      staggered lunch hour
      flexitime

8. What do workers do about lunch at present?
      (eg packed lunch, go home etc)

Preparation 1

Now read this memo about the running of a canteen and the information about the luncheon voucher scheme.

MEMO

TO: ALL STAFF   FROM: CANTEEN
                                         MANAGER

SUBJECT: REVISED CANTEEN OPERATION

In order to use the company canteen subsidy to the greatest benefit of the majority the following cost-cutting measures will come into effect from the beginning of next month:

1. The menu will still be changed daily and will be displayed in the usual way. However, choices of main course will be restricted to 3 (1 hot dish, 1 salad, 1 vegetarian dish) and the number of desserts available will be cut to 2 (1 hot and 1 cold) - fresh fruit, yoghurts and cheese will continue to be available.

2. Waitress service will be withdrawn and self-service introduced. However, a small area with waitress service will be set aside for the use of staff entertaining visitors to the company.

3. In the self-service area of the canteen all staff are asked to return all trays, dirty plates etc to the trolleys provided. Please do not leave dirty coffee/tea cups etc in the lounge area but return them to the trolleys.

4. 'Dirty jobs' employees are asked not to wear their overalls in the canteen.

5. No changes will be made to opening times for the mid-morning and mid-afternoon breaks. The canteen will open from 9.45 - 10.45 and 3.15 - 4.00, the usual choice of tea, coffee, juices, soft drinks and light snacks will be on sale.

6. There is a change in the arrangements for the lunch hour. In future, lunch will be served in two sittings: 12.30 - 1.00 and 1.15 - 1.45. Please buy your tickets for the required sitting in advance.

It is hoped that these new arrangements will lead to more cost-effective operation of the canteen without having a negative effect on either the quality of the food served or the restful atmosphere for members of staff.

These new arrangements will be monitored and a survey of opinions will be held after a period of adjustment.

The Luncheon Voucher Scheme

Employees receive a luncheon voucher for every day that they work. Because the company provides the LV's to employees free of charge, it is a good way for them to subsidise their employees' meals and provide an acceptable perk.

The company decides on the value of the voucher that they are going to give and buys them from an organisation which arranges with restaurants, sandwich bars, pubs, take-aways, cafes and shops to accept them. They can be exchanged for complete meals or for sandwiches and certain other foods. They cannot be exchanged for alcoholic drinks. A meal usually costs more than the value of a luncheon voucher but it is possible to pay the difference or use more than one voucher.

Until recently the Inland Revenue has imposed a tax on luncheon vouchers whose value was in excess of 15p a day and for this reason luncheon vouchers became less popular. However a revival may be on the way since new regulations mean that if a company has an executive dining room, then meals provided to directors can be free of charge providing that staff who are not permitted to use the executive dining room are given free or subsidised meal vouchers.

Action

In groups, discuss the merits of the two systems for your company and then choose the one which would be most suitable.

Present your decision to the other groups; you should be able to justify your choice.

7 __ Relocating The Factory

The Problem

The factory used by Morecap plc is no longer big enough. More space is needed but it is not possible to build a new factory near the present one. They must move.

The actions to be taken can be divided into 5 groups:
>   A. Preliminary work
>   B. Construction work
>   C. Work related to Customer Relations
>   D. Work related to new personnel
>   E. Work related to existing personnel

In Groups

Put these actions, necessary to relocating the factory, in the correct position on the chart:

1. Hold the opening ceremony.
2. Evaluate the information about the towns.
3. Create informative literature for all staff and customers.
4. Train new staff.
5. Have the new company stationery printed.
6. Hold a farewell presentation for the staff who are leaving the company.
7. Furnish the offices.
8. Engage an architect.
9. Move the staff that are transferring to the new factory.
10. Engage a relocation consultant.
11. Find out how many employees are going to move.
12. Arrange the levels of compensation or relocation expenses.
13. Visit the possible towns.
14. Recruit new staff.
15. Inform your customers.
16. Arrange for senior staff to see the new location.
17. Install the new production equipment.
18. Have the plans approved by the local government.
19. Have the proposals approved by the Board of Directors.
20. Write to development organisations in possible towns.
21. Draw up a short-list of towns.
22. Put the construction work out to tender.
23. Meet with the union representatives.
24. Engage a building contractor.
25. Build the factory.

>

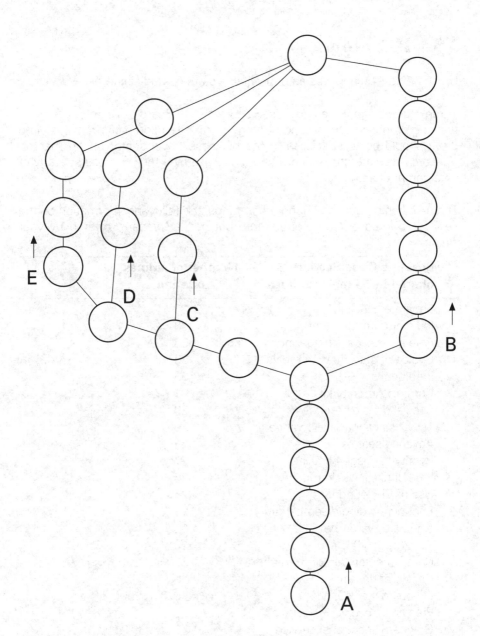

Action

Compare the solutions of different groups.

The **P**roblem

Up and Away Airlines was an unprofitable state-owned airline.

Three months ago it was privatised and the new Board of Directors decided that the proposed turn-around strategy to take the company from loss into profit should be to specialise in the business travel sector of the market. Research was therefore commissioned to examine the business strategy of your competitors.

The research produced, among other things, the following information on the services offered by your competitors but not, at present, offered by your airline.

Business Class Services offered by 33 major airlines	Number of airlines offering
Separate check-in	33
In-flight entertainment	33
Free newspapers/magazines	33
Choice of starters with meals	33
Free drinks	33
Comfort/Amenity kit	31
Special diets catered for	29
1st Class baggage allowance	29
Advance seat selection	28
Priority baggage handling	27
Free drinks incl. champagne	26
Use of VIP lounge	25
Priority boarding/disembarkation	23
On-board wardrobe	18
Passenger gift	10
Complimentary airport transfer	10
Choice of desserts	9
On-board mail service	9
Free cabin bag	5
On-board secretarial service	3
On-board telephone/fax	2

You will be given one of these roles:
    Finance Manager
    Marketing Manager
    Personnel and Training Manager

>

In Groups

Get together in pairs or small groups with the other Managers with the SAME responsibility ie. the Finance Managers in pairs or small groups, the Marketing Managers in pairs or small groups and the same with the Personnel and Training Managers.

Decide which of the above services could be introduced immediately and which need time to introduce.

Then discuss each of the services mentioned paying special attention to its impact on the department assigned to you and fill in the worksheet.
For example:
- Finance Managers should decide whether capital investment is required or whether there would only be recurring costs.

- Marketing Managers should decide whether each service would give scope for advertising or make an impact on passenger comfort.

- Personnel and Training Managers should decide whether recruitment is required or if retraining is necessary.

Action

Now form groups of 3. There should be 1 Marketing Manager, 1 Finance Manager and 1 Personnel and Training Manager in each group.

Finally decide on what recommendations should be made to the Board as far as introducing new services is concerned.
Take into account the following:
As no single airline offers all these services – on average 13 of the 21 listed are offered, it would seem that, to become competitive you should introduce 14 of the services: 7 should be introduced immediately and 7 within the next year.

Recommendations

1	1
2	2
3	3
4	4
5	5
6	6
7	7

SERVICES	FEASIBILITY for immediate/ non-immediate introduction	MARKETING Impact on: Advertising, Passenger comfort etc	FINANCE Impact on: Capital Invest- ment, recurring costs etc	PERSONNEL TRAINING Impact on: Recruitment, re-training etc
1. Separate check-in				
2. In-flight entertainment				
3. Free newspapers and magazines				
4. Choice of starters				
5. Free drinks				
6. Comfort/ amenity kit				
7. Special diets catered for				
8. 1st Class baggage allowance				
9. Advance seat selection				
10. Priority baggage handling				
11. Free drinks incl. champagne				
12. Use of VIP lounge				
13. Priority boarding disembarking				
14. On-board wardrobe				
15. Passenger gift				
16. Free airport transfer				
17. Choice of desserts				
18. On-board mail service				
19. Free cabin bag				
20. On-board secretarial service				
21. On-board telephone/ fax				

9 ___ Choosing a Credit Card

The Problem

Read these three advertisements for credit cards and analyse the features of each card using the ideas from the table.

SPREE   The card for you!

Now you can buy what you want, when you see it.

Holding the Spree card will cost you nothing. We will send you a statement each month and you need only pay us 10% of your total purchases or a minimum payment of £10. We will agree a credit limit with you. Don't worry if you lose your Spree card – for a small charge we will insure it so that you have zero liability for unauthorised use.

The number of shops, restaurants, garages etc. accepting the Spree card is increasing each month.

Interest is charged only from the final date for payment shown on your statement. If you need cash, then you can get that too – but we have to charge interest from the date of withdrawal.

HAPPIBUY   Become a happy buyer!

It will cost you only £8 a year to get your Happibuy card and you can have an extra card for another member of your family absolutely free. We send you a monthly statement and no interest is payable if you send us a cheque for the total balance within 2 weeks. Losing your Happibuy is not a big problem – report the loss to us and you have no liability after that.

Happibuy is becoming more and more popular with shoppers and shop keepers. It is easy to get and easy to use. Most shops nationwide accept the Happibuy card and we can make arrangements for you to use it abroad if you wish – a small fee is all that is required.

You can withdraw cash from specified cash dispensers and buy travellers' cheques from certain travel agents. With these transactions interest has to be charged from the date of the transaction. We give you an initial credit limit of up to £500.

SPENDFLEX   We have the answers!

1. Where can I use my Spendflex card?
Spendflex is the nation's most widely accepted card and it is expanding rapidly all over the world.

2. What interest do I pay?
If you clear your account when you receive your statement then you pay no interest, otherwise we charge interest at the rate of 1% over minimum lending rate on your outstanding balance each month.

3. Can a member of my family share the same account?
You can specify up to three additional people to use your account. Each has a separate card and a separate credit limit.

4. What payments do I have to make?
You must pay at least 5% of your month's balance within 7 days.

5. Can I get travellers' cheques or cash with my Spendflex card?
We can provide other services such as cash withdrawal and purchase of travellers' cheques – ask for details of these facilities and also for the small annual charge that we make for the convenience of having our card.
Remember – More people have Spendflex than any other card.

In Groups

Analyse the information and fill in this table:

	Spree	Spendflex	Happibuy
Cost of card			
Obtain cash			
Extra cards			
Statements			
Minimum monthly repayments			
Interest free period			
Credit limit			
Use nationwide/ worldwide			

Action

The following people want a credit card – use your analysis of the three credit cards to discuss and decide which card you think would be best in each case:

John Lerner is a medical student. He is in his final year at college and in 4 months time will start working in his first job. Although he will have a room provided in the hospital he hopes to rent a flat to live in when he is not on duty in the hospital.

He has a girlfriend but he has no plans to marry at present.

Peter and Mary Kuple were married 9 months ago and are finding balancing their budget quite difficult.

Their income varies each month depending on the amount of overtime that Peter works. Mary has a part-time job.

Stephen Driver is one of three salesmen for his company and he travels to see clients both in this country and abroad. He has to submit a monthly expense account to his company. Because he travels so much he prefers not to carry too much cash but he finds that many hotels are often not happy to put extras on the bill.

Paul and Susan Middle have 2 children who are away from home at university and have to pay most of their children's living expenses. Paul has a good job with an international company as Personnel Manager at their Welsh factory. They have a country cottage about 200 miles from their home where they spend most of their holidays.

When you have had your discussion, you will have to report on your analysis of the cards and present your decisions – justifying them if necessary.

The **P**roblem

This is a negotiation between an Office Services Manager and a Trade Union Representative. When you have read about the work of Office Services Departments in general and the specific points raised by the staff in this particular company, you will be given a role and also some extra information to help you to negotiate.

The Office Services Department

The job of the Office Services Department is to keep the company's buildings clean and in good repair and also to make sure that the employees have a good environment to work in. It looks after the general comfort of the company's staff, making sure that their surroundings and equipment comply with health and safety laws and allow them to work as efficiently as possible. Everything has to be maintained and, from time to time, replaced and so the OSD has to obtain information for all departments which need new office furniture and equipment.

In **P**airs

In pairs make a list of some of the cleaning / maintenance / purchasing installation enquiry / work which an Office Services Department may have to organise.

———————————————————————————————

———————————————————————————————

———————————————————————————————

The **M**eeting

A meeting has been arranged between the Office Services Department and the Trade Union Shop Stewards to discuss and find solutions to the following points that have been raised by the staff.

1. Complaints of headaches, said to be due to poor or wrong lighting.
2. Canteen queues are too long.
3. Staircases and corridors are dark and drab.
4. People working with VDU's suffer from tiredness and headaches.
5. Workers on the south side of the building are insufferably hot in summer, when the sun comes in.
6. Department heads have complained that staff are late more often than they used to be. The most frequent excuse is that buses are full and the staff have to wait for several buses before they get on one.
7. Many complaints of backache from staff who sit all day.

Trade Union Representative

Special information for the Trade Union Representatives — the management must not know that you have this information.

In order to prepare for your negotiation, form a group with the other Trade Union Representatives and read about your role.

Your main objective is to get the complaints dealt with as quickly as possible. There are four months of this financial year left and you have been told that there is still money in the Office Services budget as yet unspent.

REMEMBER — The management must not know that you have this information.

Discuss the possible solutions to each complaint with the others in your group and decide which you will press for when you meet the management.

Form a pair with an Office Services Manager and role play the meeting in pairs.

Office Services Manager

Special information for the Office Services Managers — it would be undiplomatic if you told this to the Trade Union Representatives.

In order to prepare for your negotiation, form a group with the other Office Services Managers and read about your role.

There are 4 months of this financial year left but the remainder of your budget is promised for the total renovation of the Managing Director's office suite.

REMEMBER — It would be most undiplomatic to tell this to the Union Representatives.

Discuss the possible solutions to each complaint with the others in your group and decide which you will suggest when you meet the union.

Form a pair with a Trade Union Representative and role play the meeting in pairs.

11 _____ Business Entertaining

The Problem

About £700m a year is spent by companies on corporate hospitality, not only on business lunches etc. to discuss or finalise a contract but on entertainment with no specific objective in mind except to keep or win the loyalty of clients.

In the past three years your company has always used a 'hospitality broker' who would arrange a visit to a social or sporting occasion to which your executives could invite and entertain selected valued clients.

Unfortunately last year it was not as successful as in previous years and so, this year, the arrangements are to be made internally – in fact, by you.

There are a number of alternatives – you may like to think of others:

Sporting Events which are also Social Events	British Open Golf Championship Wimbledon Horse Racing (The Derby or Grand National) British Grand Prix An International Rugby match
Participation Sports	Shooting in Yorkshire(grouse/pheasant) Salmon Fishing(Scotland/Ireland) Clay Pigeon Shooting Motor Racing Use of a Skid Pan War Games
Weekend away	Scottish Castle Country House City Hotel Skiing in the Alps
Trip to an unusual place/ event	North Pole By Concorde to a Broadway Show Football World Cup Olympic Games
Dinner + West End Show	
Other Special Event	

In Pairs

Consider the value and the limitations of these ideas.

Consider: danger/effect on health
                 expense
                 time required (weekend/weekday/evening)
                 possibility/desirability of inviting spouses/partners
                 exclusivity/non-exclusivity
                 ease of arrangement/possibility of things going wrong
                 level of enjoyment
                 level of stimulation
                 previous experience required
                 physical ability required
and any other points that you think important.

Now make a group with 2 or 3 others and compare ideas.

Then create the profile of the clients that you have to entertain.
Consider:-

AGE RANGE _____ **NATIONALITY** _____

OCCUPATIONS _____

_____

POSSIBLE INTERESTS _____

_____

TIME AVAILABLE _____

OTHER FACTORS _____

_____

Action

Finally discuss and decide what you are going to organise for them.
Each group will have to present the profile of their clients and explain their
decision – this includes explaining why other alternatives were rejected.

12 ——————— **J**oining the **T**eam

The **P**roblem

You are the manager of the British Athletics team due to go to the World Championships in 2 months time.

Yesterday the national qualifying competition was held. The stated intention was that the athletes who performed best would automatically be chosen for the team, making the choice of the team simpler and less controversial.

Two British women are permitted to compete in the women's 1,000 metres in the Championships. The choice of Dawn Jones who came first in the qualifying race is clear and creates no problems. She has been in excellent form this season and has always done well in previous international competitions.

Who should be the second British competitor is not so easy as there are 2 athletes with good claims to being the second member of the team.

In **G**roups

To start with you will work in 2 groups.

Each group will be given information about only one of the 2 athletes. Follow the instructions on the information sheet so that you can collect everything you need to know about both athletes.

Then you will be able to discuss which athlete should join the team and make a well-informed choice.

>

Group **1**

Mary Locker

Mary Locker is 25. She was born in Britain and is the present World Record Holder for both the 1,000 and 3,000 metres.

During this season she has suffered from an injury that has interrupted her training programme. However, she is now back in training and in her last three races her time has improved on each occasion.
She was the winner of the last World Championships and won a Gold Medal at last year's Olympic Games.
Every time that she has represented her country her performance has always been excellent and she has always won a medal.
In the qualifying competition she came fourth.

In your group, first summarise the information that you have about your athlete and then make a list of questions that you need to ask so that you will be able to compare the 2 athletes.

_____

_____

_____

_____

_____

In **P**airs

Make a pair with someone who knows about the other athlete, Jean Flower. In your pair ask and answer questions so that you both have full information about both athletes.

Then discuss and decide what you should do, remembering the stated intention of the qualifying competition, and that you do not want problems either with other countries which might result in the cancellation of the Championships, or with other British athletes, or with the British media.

Which athlete should represent Britain in the Championships?

Group 2

Jean Flower

Jean Flower is 19 with no experience in international competitions. She was not born in Britain but took out British citizenship 6 months ago because the country that she was born and lived in was subject to a boycott from international competitions.

Until 6 months ago her performances had been excellent, in fact, either just above or even just below the world record time. Naturally they were not recognised because of the boycott. After her arrival in Britain she was off-form, probably as a result of the public controversy about her change of nationality and the adverse publicity in the media.

This has included a threat by some countries not to take part in the Championships if Jean Flower is a member of the British team.

In the qualifying competition she came second.

In your group, first summarise the information that you have about your athlete and then make a list of questions that you need to ask so that you will be able to compare the 2 athletes.

_____

_____

_____

_____

_____

In Pairs

Make a pair with someone who knows about the other athlete, Mary Locker. In your pair ask and answer questions so that you both have full information about both athletes.

Then discuss and decide what you should do, remembering the stated intention of the qualifying competition, and that you do not want problems either with other countries which might result in the cancellation of the Championships, or with other British athletes, or with the British media.

Which athlete should represent Britain in the Championships?

The **P**roblem

Group 1

You are a radio DJ (disc jockey) and have been asked to put together a record album which will be sold in aid of Famine-Aid (famine relief in Africa). If the album is to be in the shops in time to take advantage of the lucrative pre-Christmas market, you need to get the musicians into the recording studio within the next two weeks.

The line-up of artists prepared to give their time is almost complete but you need one more track and so, one more band. You have to decide which of two bands to ask. Here is information about one of the bands.

The Streetcreds

'The Streetcreds' are a group of 4 (1 woman – the vocalist – and 3 men on keyboard, drums and guitar). They come from America but spend much of their time in Britain. At present they are on an international tour which does not finish for another 3 weeks.

When they are on tour they always give the proceeds of 1 of their concerts to charity. They have done 5 tours worldwide including 1 in China.

The Streetcreds' last UK appearance was 4 months ago at Wembley Stadium and it was a sell out within 24 hours of the box office opening. The album of this gig, recorded live, is due to be released in 2 months.

They have had 10 Number 1 hits and their latest single release went into the charts at Number 3 and stayed 4 weeks at Number 1. It won a Golden Disc at the Geneva Festival and the video broke all sales records.

In your group, first summarise the information that you have about 'The Streetcreds' and then make a list of questions that you need to ask so that you will be able to compare the 2 bands.

Action

Make a pair with someone who knows about the other band, 'Cuz'. In your pair ask and answer questions so that you both have full information about both bands. Then discuss and decide which band you will ask to record the last track for your album.

The Problem

Group 2

You are a radio DJ (disc jockey) and have been asked to put together a record album which will be sold in aid of Famine-Aid (famine relief in Africa). If the album is to be in the shops in time to take advantage of the lucrative pre-Christmas market, you need to get the musicians into the recording studio within the next two weeks.

The line-up of artists prepared to give their time is almost complete but you need one more track and so, one more band.

You have to decide which of two bands to ask. Here is information about one of the bands.

'Cuz'

'Cuz' is a group of 3 men, a lead vocalist who also plays the guitar, a drummer and a sax player, all from Britain. They are at present on a tour of the UK and although their concerts were not well attended at the beginning of the tour, the audiences are increasing and the press are becoming more enthusiastic. Their previous tour was as the support group for the famous Bill Collins.

Cuz's latest single release rose to Number 2 in the UK Charts but they have never made Number 1. They have just signed a 2-year contract, with a possible 5-year extension, with Burgin Records, a small, little known company.

They have never done a charity performance. Last year they said they were unable to do a record in aid of homeless people.

At last year's Reading Pop Festival their drummer was arrested for possessing drugs and they were unable to fulfill their contract. Their manager says that they could be available for 2 days next week between live appearances.

In your group, first summarise the information that you have about 'Cuz' and then make a list of questions that you need to ask so that you will be able to compare the 2 bands.

Action

Make a pair with someone who knows about the other band, 'The Streetcreds'. In your pair ask and answer questions so that you both have full information about both bands. Then discuss and decide which band you will ask to record the last track for your album.

14 ___ **E**mployee **D**evelopment

The **P**roblem

Company Profile

Suave Ltd is a busy manufacturing company. They produce men's shirts in a highly competitive market. At the moment they export about 40% of their production and they know that, in the current economic climate, increasing exports is the most promising growth area for their business and a new export sales manager is soon to be created. Two years ago Suave Ltd were taken over by a forward-looking company, a fabric manufacturer whose business complements theirs.

Since the takeover many changes have been made, including the introduction of computer-assisted cutting equipment. This has resulted in an increase in production but with no increase in the amount of fabric used. There has, therefore, been an increase in profits.

The parent company encourages a generous budget for training, both for shop-floor workers and for management.

In **G**roups

Look at the information about possible courses for senior management and decide who you would send on a course and which course you would choose. (You can choose more than one manager and more than one course if you wish.)

Consider the following executives for courses:

Decision Grid

	Needs	Course
Managing Director		
Production Manager		
Finance Manager		
Personnel Manager		
Export Sales Manager		
Domestic Sales Manager		
Other		

>

Course One: Effective Speaking

Length of Course: 1 day

Topics Covered: Planning and giving a presentation
Selecting and using visual aids
Presenting arguments / ideas persuasively
Managing nerves
Keeping the audience interested
Dealing with questions confidently

Who should attend:
Most managers will benefit from this course particularly those who need to present an idea confidently and effectively to any number of people.

Course Two: Effective Meetings

Length of Course: 1 day

Topics Covered: Preparing an agenda
Room layout and seating
Effective visual aids
Managing time during the meeting
Lubricating discussion
Contributing effectively
Follow up

Who should attend:
Anyone who participates in meetings, runs meetings, or takes part in decision making.

Course Three: Recruitment Interviewing Skills

Length of Course: 1 day

Topics Covered: Preparation of the job description
Comparing the different advertising methods
Defining the ideal candidate
Preparing for the interview
Making an interview plan and conducting the interview
Behavioural skills and body language
Evaluating the success of interview methods

Who should attend:
Anyone who has to choose new staff to join their organisation and wants to make sure that they choose the best person for the job.

Course Four: Building and Leading a Team

Length of Course: 2 days

Topics Covered: Choosing and motivating a good team
Creating an atmosphere which produces good teamwork
Identifying and eliminating factors which reduce good teamwork
Using individual strengths
Improving communication within the team
Leadership skills
Producing an action plan and monitoring it

Who should attend:
Newly-appointed team leaders or managers. Managers whose success is likely to be affected by the performance of their team and teamwork.

Course Five: Time Management

Length of Course: 2 linked days with 3 weeks in between

Topics Covered: Analysing how time is spent
Deciding on priorities and allocating time
Identifying time-wasters and eliminating them
Delegation
Controlling workload, paperwork and interruptions
Your diary/personal organiser

Who should attend:
All who want to achieve more in less time and who want practical ideas and techniques that they can apply immediately.

Course Six: Stress Management

Length of Course: 2 days

Topics Covered: Understanding stress and how to use it as a motivator
Positive stress reduction strategies
Avoiding negative strategies such as drink and drugs
Relaxation techniques
Practical ways of managing stress to maintain and improve effective performance in yourself and others

Who should attend:
All those who may be under stress themselves or who have managerial responsibility for sustaining the performance or motivation of staff.

15 ⎯⎯⎯⎯⎯ **S**elling **I**nstanews

The **P**roblem

Group 1

You work for Instanews, an electronic screen-delivered information service which transmits a wide variety of regularly up-dated information.
One of your potential clients is an international hotel chain with 15 hotels in big cities nationwide and 10 others worldwide.

Below there are details of half of the information services that Instanews transmits. Read it carefully with other members of Group 1.

TRAVEL NEWS	WEATHER REPORTS	AIR TRAVEL UPDATE
Road, rail, sea	Today's weather	All about your nearest airport
Timetable changes Delays Motorway problems Traffic jams Road works	Short term and long term forecasts	Timetable updates Arrivals/departures Car park advice Travel news/advice
DISH OF THE DAY	**CHART TOPPERS**	**HOBBIES NEWS**
A recipe for today Full instructions Where to get your ingredients	Pop music Videos Classical music Books etc	Tips for Gardening and DIY Photography, Painting etc
Changed daily		
SPORTS SERVICE	**FARMING NEWS**	**SHOPPING TROLLEY**
Results Service	Weather Prices	Services offered by local traders, opening times
Sports events national/local dates and times	Farm Shop News	Bargains

In **P**airs

Now find a partner from Group 2 who will have the rest of the information which you need. Ask and answer questions so that both of you collect full information.

Action

Join up with another pair to make a group to discuss and decide on the services most likely to interest your client either in the running of their hotel chain or for their hotel guests. Be ready to explain your choice and give good reasons why your client should install your service.

>

The Problem

Group 2

You work for Instanews, an electronic screen-delivered information service which transmits a wide variety of regularly up-dated information.
One of your potential clients is an international hotel chain with 15 hotels in big cities nationwide and 10 others worldwide.

Below there are details of half of the information services that Instanews transmits. Read it carefully with other members of Group 2.

THEATRES, CINEMAS CONCERTS, DISCOS	FINANCIAL MARKETS	LOCAL INFORMATION
What's on Reviews	Stock Exchange Foreign Exchange rates	Library times Evening classes
Performance times Seat availability	Regular updates	News from local clubs
TOURIST INFORMATION	**RESTAURANTS AND PUBS**	**CURRENT AFFAIRS**
What to do Where to go	Addresses Opening times Menus	News as it happens National and International
Opening times Entrance fees Transport advice	Phone numbers for booking	Press Agency Reports What the papers say
RADIO AND TV	**BUSINESS NEWS**	**CHILDRENS CORNER**
Satellite, Non-satellite local/national	Company news	Games, puzzles, Books
Times and wavelengths	National and local Job vacancies	Fashion etc

In Pairs

Now find a partner from Group 1 who will have the rest of the information which you need. Ask and answer questions so that both of you collect full information.

Action

Join up with another pair to make a group to discuss and decide on the services most likely to interest your client either in the running of their hotel chain or for their hotel guests. Be ready to explain your choice and give good reasons why your client should install your service.

16 _____ **A**ppointment **B**oard

The **P**roblem

Archer Electronics, a family company, was founded 40 years ago by Daniel Archer who retired 5 years ago from being the Managing Director. However, he still takes an active interest in the development and changes in the company and he is now a non-executive director and holds 33.3% of the shares of the company. 10 years ago he married his second wife, formerly Ann Fund, who was and still is, the Finance Manager of the company. As a wedding present she received 33.3% of the company's shares.

The present Managing Director of the company, Michael Brett, is married to Daniel Archer's only daughter Jean who is also a non-executive director of the company and who also holds 33.3% of the shares.

Recently Archer Electronics has been expanding and investing in new technology. A new Warehousing Department is to be created and it will be responsible for controlling in-coming stock and distributing the end product. This department will be under the control of the Production Manager, Geoff Butcher, who is also a member of the Board.

A new computer system is to be installed in the Warehousing Department with new software not previously used by the company. 2 identical jobs working with the computer are still vacant. They have been widely advertised both internally and externally and on the short-list of 4 are: Andrew Bolton, Brian Underwood, Claude Fund and David Campbell.

In the circumstances, and also because Archer Electronics is a family firm, the short-list is to be considered by a working party which has been created to oversee the setting-up of the new department.

First draw the organigram of Archer Electronics' Board of Directors:

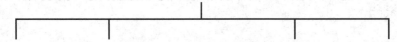

Action

Now read the information about the 4 candidates. In pairs analyse their good points, bad points and any other relevant information. You will be given a role and asked to role play a meeting of the appointment board to recommend which two candidates should be appointed.

The Candidates

Andrew Bolton, aged 27, is a university graduate. After graduating he spent 2 years at Archer Electronics and then 2 years ago he left to join another electronics company where he worked in their computerised stock control department.

He is enthusiastic, well-liked, hard-working and works well in a team.

In the last year he has been attending a communication skills evening class.

He is about to get married – his fiancee has a responsible job in the marketing department of a big multi-national company.

His present salary is slightly above average and also above the salary range that you are offering.

Brian Underwood is 40, attended technical college until he was 18 and then joined Archer Electronics. He has been working in the stock control section for 20 years and because of the re-organisation, has applied for a transfer. In fact, with the re-organisation, there is no longer a job for him and he may have to be made redundant*.

He is a reliable worker, although he prefers to work on his own. He always leaves at 5 o'clock on the dot. He has been offered a place on 'skill development' courses twice but has refused each time 'for family reasons'.

He has 2 children under 10 and took out a mortgage on a house a year ago.

Six months ago his wife was made redundant by Archers when the production process she worked on was automated.

David Campbell is 58 and has also applied for transfer from the section that used to be in charge of stock control. He joined Archer Electronics when he left school at 16.

There is no suitable job for him in the Production Department and he will have to be made redundant if not appointed to this job.*

He is a good and efficient worker but panics under stress.

He recently raised a big loan on his house so that he could send his daughter to university and also make changes to his house so that he can accommodate his son who is handicapped after a car crash in which his (David's) wife was killed.

Claude Fund is 30 and the son of Ann Archer by her first marriage.

He is a university graduate and speaks several languages. He used to work for a computer company as a customer engineer, helping users to solve their problems.

At his last job he had a reputation for being lazy and difficult to work with. He frequently asked other people to do his work. He was disliked by his colleagues and clients.

He will inherit his mother's 33.3% share in the company when she dies.

* Redundancy pay depends both on salary and length of service so that the longer the time with the company then the higher the redundancy pay.

17 Strengths and Weaknesses

The Problem

In pairs, draw a typical organigram of a manufacturing company. You can choose the company's name, what it makes and how and where it operates but it has to include everyone who works in the company – not only the managers but also the secretaries, production workers, salesmen and supervisors etc.

Organigram of _____ Products _____

In Groups

Then you will be given information about the characteristics of people born under various signs of the Zodiac. You will work in 3 groups. Each group will receive information about 4 different signs. Total 12 signs in all. Read the information carefully.

Find 2 other people both with different information from yours and complete your information by asking and answering questions.

Next, in this group of 3 look at each of the Zodiac signs, decide which of the characteristics mentioned are important in the world of work (either positively or negatively).

Now for each Zodiac sign make a list of the characteristics.

Aries	+ −	Libra	+ −
Taurus	+ −	Scorpio	+ −
Gemini	+ −	Sagittarius	+ −
Cancer	+ −	Capricorn	+ −
Leo	+ −	Aquarius	+ −
Virgo	+ −	Pisces	+ −

Action

Then discuss and decide which jobs in the company should be done by which people from which Zodiac sign(s).

Information **S**heet **A**

Aries   21 March to 20 April

Courageous leaders, energetic, ambitious, lovers of new ideas, have a desire for quick results, impatient, insensitive to others, manipulative, quick-witted, unable to foresee difficulties, self-centred, unwilling to obey, punctual, prone to accidents and physical injury, over-optimistic.

Taurus   21 April to 20 May

Hostile to change, industrious, reliable, practical, methodical, lazy, dislike exercise, creative, good founders of enterprises, work best in routine positions of trust and responsibility, horror of debt, good with their hands, enjoy music and art, love good food and luxury, practical rather than intellectual, fixed opinions, over-cautious.

Gemini   21 May to 21 June

Versatile, able to see both sides of a question, take on too many projects, childish, demand others' time and energy, like life to be exciting and free of routine, kind, generous, don't take things seriously, worriers, intelligent, enjoy learning new things, good communicators, sometimes liars or confidence tricksters.

Cancer   22 June to 22 July

Thick-skinned, unemotional, insensitive, intuitive, good memories, sympathetic, imaginative, determined, change opinions and loyalties easily, tactless, easily corrupted, moody, difficult, sometimes have an inferiority complex, a good sense of money, idealistic, easily flattered, good at looking after others.

Notes

_____

_____

_____

_____

Action

When you have information about people from the other 8 zodiac signs, discuss and decide which jobs in the company should be done by people from which sign(s).

Information **S**heet **B**

Leo   23 July to 22 August

Natural leaders, outgoing, outspoken, enthusiastic, inspire loyalty in others, practical, cheerful, brave, creative, dignified, delegate details, love pleasure and luxury, arrogant, intolerant, impetuous, suspicious of rivals.

Virgo   23 August to 22 September

Dignified, charming, quiet, not very friendly, sensible, discrete, understand others' problems, enjoy learning, good with their hands, logical, analytical, easily discouraged, accept new ideas, careful with money, like routine, pay attention to detail, worriers, hypochondriacs, make mountains out of molehills.

Libra   23 September to 22 October

Elegant, kind, hate cruelty, optimistic, co-operative, love harmony, hate conflict, artistic rather than scholarly, observant, dislike extremes, trustworthy with other people's money, women can be careless with money, over-enthusiastic for new causes, don't like being criticised, don't like dirty work, sometimes ambitious, want approval.

Scorpio   23 October to 22 November

Unconventional, courteous, dignified, reserved, thoughtful in conversation, strong will-power, sensitive, quick to anger, religious, vindictive, love to be praised and flattered, discard friends when they are no longer useful, procrastinators.

Notes

_____

_____

_____

_____

Action

When you have information about people from the other 8 zodiac signs, discuss and decide which jobs in the company should be done by people from which sign(s).

>

Information **S**heet **C**

Sagittarius   23 November to 22 December

Idealistic, optimistic, generous, fair-minded, versatile, forgiving, religious, foresighted, good judgement, innovative, restless, ambitious, want to be leaders, enjoy travel, tactless, inconsiderate, quick-tempered, rush plans through immediately, expect too much of others, demand recognition for themselves, neglectful of their duties.

Capricorn   23 December to 20 January

Serious, hard-working, persistent, over-cautious, economical with money, independent, achieve great results with minimum effort, can do several things at the same time, determined, resourceful, good organisers, respect discipline, good memories, lack originality, family life is important, selfish, pessimistic, practical business ability combined with tact.

Aquarius   21 January to 19 February

Quiet, gentle, strong-willed, speak moderately, idealistic, don't respect authority, intelligent, inventive, logical thinkers, able to change their opinions if evidence shows they are wrong, make few friends, good judges of human nature, work well in a team, secretive, break promises.

Pisces   20 February to 20 March

Dislike discipline, imaginative, versatile, popular with all kinds of people, easy-going, honest, let problems solve themselves rather than trying to solve them, they give more than they ask, loyal, home-loving, sympathetic, unreliable, gossipers, careless, impractical, indecisive in important matters, dependent on others, can turn to drink and drugs.

Notes

_____
_____
_____
_____

Action

When you have information about people from the other 8 zodiac signs, discuss and decide which jobs in the company should be done by people from which sign(s).

18 _____ T rade F air V enue

T he P roblem

You are a project manager for Confix, a company specialising in arranging conferences and conventions.

You have to organise a Trade Fair for organisations who train people in using all forms of new technology. The Trade Fair has to attract people from all over the world both as exhibitors and visitors.

I n P airs

Discuss and decide what amenities are important in the city where the Trade Fair will be held. Consider these points and fill in Table 1:

Table 1

	Delegates' Needs
The city (Historic / Industrial)	
The weather	
Transport (to the city)	
Transport (in the city)	
Food / Restaurants	
Hotels	
Entertainment(theatres,cinemas etc.)	
Shopping facilities	
Opportunities for sightseeing	
The country (developed / 3rd world)	

I n G roups

Now you will be given information about various venues and the facilities that they offer. You will start by dividing into 2 groups.
Each group will be given information about 3 of the 6 possible venues.
Read the information carefully and, in pairs, summarise it and fill in as much as you can of Table 2.

I n P airs

Now exchange information with someone who had information about the other 3 venues and fill in the rest of Table 2.

A ction

Finally choose the Trade Fair Venue according to the needs of the client defined at the bottom of your 'Information on Venues' sheet.

Calgary, Canada

The convention centre was opened 2 years ago at a cost of £1 billion with an auditorium for 3,500, restaurant facilities for 2,200, plus 20 other meeting rooms for between 100 and 620 people. It has a concert hall for 2,500, a theatre for 500, plus an exhibition area of 3,000 square metres. Calgary is a rapidly developing city with an efficient bus and underground system. It is home to the annual 'Stampede' which attracts 1.5 million visitors every year.

Nairobi, Kenya

Nairobi is the centre of the East African safari tourist trade which is at its peak between November and April. The Koi Conference Complex is due to be opened in 2 months time at a cost of £30 million. It is designed to house sport, music, trade fairs and conventions. The large assembly hall will seat 9,000 delegates with an additional 5 conference rooms accommodating a total of 6,500. It is a multi-purpose building in the centre of the capital of a rapidly developing 3rd World nation. It has 5,000 square metres of exhibition space.

London, UK

The East London (Docklands) Conference Centre which opened in February can host events with audiences of up to 12,600. The seating can easily be moved to provide 7,900 square metres of exhibition space. Other rooms can accommodate between 70 and 400 people. Docklands has a newly-built railway link with the City and other areas of London. There is a wide range of hotel accommodation in the West and Central London area.

Action

Collect information about the other 3 possible venues. FINALLY choose the best venue for the Trade Fair. You will have to explain your choice to the committee of organisers.

Your clients want:
a) to accomodate at least 150 exhibitors
b) to hold an opening dinner for 1,500 people (exhibitors, visitors, local business people, government representatives, etc.)
c) to offer smaller meeting rooms for exhibitors to have meetings with possible clients
d) to offer exhibitors good facilities for entertaining visitors
e) video-conferencing facilities
f) the most modern technological aids (sound / visual systems etc.)
g) to attract the maximum number of visitors

Hawaii, US

The Convention and Exhibition Centre was opened last year with a conference hall for 2,600. It has other meeting rooms with capacities ranging from 40 to 600. Facilities include modern sound equipment, theatre lighting and simultaneous translation. The total exhibition space is 22,700 square metres divided into 3 areas. Hawaii has a worldwide reputation as a beautiful island and a tourist centre.

Paris, France

The conference centre which opened this year in Paris – the food capital of the world – is an extension of existing facilities. The combined complex will accommodate 5,000, with one auditorium seating 1,000, another for 700 and a third for 350. In addition there are several smaller meeting rooms with capacities ranging from 20 to 100. One auditorium can easily be adapted to provide an exhibition area for 130 stands. Another can be adapted to provide banqueting facilities. The centre can provide all the usual exhibition and conference equipment. The Paris Metro is now one of the most modern city transport systems in the world with high speed lines to areas outside the city centre.

Saporro, Japan

The International Conference Centre was opened just over a year ago. The main hall will seat 3,000 and there are 16 other meeting rooms with capacities ranging from 40 to 1,000. Equipment provides for simultaneous translation, audio-visual presentations and many other features. The nearby Palace and Yokosaki Hotels provide excellent accommodation. Video-conferencing facilities should be fully operational within the next 6 months.

Action

Collect information about the other 3 possible venues. FINALLY choose the best venue for the Trade Fair. You will have to explain your choice to the committee of organisers.

Your clients want:
a) to accomodate at least 150 exhibitors
b) to hold an opening dinner for 1,500 people (exhibitors, visitors, local business people, government representatives, etc.)
c) to offer smaller meeting rooms for exhibitors to have meetings with possible clients
d) to offer exhibitors good facilities for entertaining visitors
e) video-conferencing facilities
f) the most modern technological aids (sound / visual systems etc.)
g) to attract the maximum number of visitors

Table 2

	Calgary Canada	Hawaii US	London UK	Nairobi Kenya	Paris France	Saporro Japan
Exhibition space						
Banqueting facilities						
Seminar rooms						
Transport facilities						
Hotels						
Restaurant facilities						
Video facilities						
Special equipment						
Other facilities						

The **P**roblem

As members of one of the PR teams of Gatebridge Council you are going to be presenting information at a public exhibition. First read this background information and then you will be given details of your special part in this exhibition.

From: Transport Dept.
To: Design and Planning/Operations Dept.

The traffic in the city of Gatebridge is grinding to a halt because the majority of people use cars to travel about the city. This is due, in some part, to the lack of an efficient public transport system.

The decision has been taken to build a 30-mile underground rail network designed to serve, not only Gatebridge, but also the nearby towns of Newland and Suncastle (1.75 million people in all). There will be 20 stations on the network, 18 miles of which will be underground and 12 miles above-ground. When completed it will be the most advanced underground system in the world. A similar one has been built in northern France but the system has been further developed and any teething troubles solved.

The system will be fully automated including the ticket selling and barriers and the trains will be driverless. The stations will be light, airey, artistically designed and easy to keep clean. There will be 300 cameras located on the platforms, in booking halls and on trains and they will feed back through a mainframe computer to a central control centre where there are 30 monitor screens manned by 10 people.

The carriages are designed to be aerodynamic and also pleasant and comfortable to travel in. They have a sleek shape, made of aluminium and have automatic glass doors. When compared with the Metro trains in Paris they are narrower and shorter (6.75 ft wide and 42.6 ft long as opposed to 8 ft wide and 49.2 ft long for the Paris Metro). In the rush hour the trains will be made up of 3 carriages carrying a total of 186 people and run every minute. Outside the rush hour the trains will have 2 carriages and run one every 5 minutes.

Because of the design of the carriages and the fact that the system is computer-controlled the trains are expected to travel faster than other systems - 22.4 mph (average speed) compared with 15.5 mph in Paris. Running costs should be lower and the smaller train size means that construction costs for tunnels and bridges will be lower.

Although fewer staff will be needed than in non-automatic systems, care has been taken to provide a high level of both safety and security. Sensors will detect if there is anything on the line which might cause an accident and trains will be stopped while the sensors diagnose the problem. An average delay of 10 seconds is expected before the train can proceed as soon as the sensors decide that all is well. As far as security is concerned, a 30-strong force will respond immediately to any problems which are observed on the monitor screens or which are communicated to the control centre by passengers using the telephones located on the trains, on the platforms or in booking halls.

>

Design and Planning Team
In Groups

The City Council are preparing a display and presentation to inform the people of Gatebridge, Newland and Suncastle about the new underground rail network, its technological achievement and the benefits to the city.

You are the PR team in the Design and Planning Department.

From the background information that you have read, extract what is relevant to your department under the following headings:

Areas covered

_____

Length of line

_____

Comparison with the Paris Metro

_____

Economic information about the design

_____

Design of stations

_____

Passenger capacity

_____

Action

Now prepare a presentation – use maps, comparative diagrams or representations of the given figures and information. Make it as interesting and easy to understand as possible.

Operations Team

In Groups

The City Council are preparing a display and presentation to inform the people of Gatebridge, Newland and Suncastle about the new underground rail network, its technological achievement and the benefits to the city.

You are the PR team in the Operations Department.

From the background information that you have read, extract what is relevant to your department.

Population served

_____

Number of stations

_____

Frequency of trains

_____

Safety features

_____

Security features

_____

Manning of trains and stations

_____

Control of the trains

_____

Action

Now prepare a presentation – use diagrams or graphic representations of the given figures and information. Make it as interesting and easy to understand as possible.

Section 2   Business Issues

1. Company Training

What problems might a company have which could be solved by a training programme?
What are the general benefits to a company and employees of a good training programme?

2. Profit-Sharing

The profitability of your company is improving and you want to share this with your employees.
Suggest possible schemes to achieve this.
Which schemes are better for the company and which schemes are better for the employees?

3. Supplying Demand

Demand for your product is greater than your present retail outlets can cope with.
What possible methods are there of increasing your sales and what are the advantages and disadvantages of the various possibilities?

4. Falling Sales

Sales of your product are declining. What might be the possible causes and what could be done to reverse the decline?

5. Relocation?

Your present manufacturing plant cannot cope with demand and there is no chance of expansion in the area where you are located at present.
What are the pros and cons of total relocation as opposed to getting additional facilities elsewhere?
What points should you consider when choosing the new location?

6. Raising Capital

You are a family firm which needs capital to finance the production of a revolutionary new product.
What possible methods are there of raising the money and what are their advantages and disadvantages to the family?

7. Protecting Your Market Share

Although sales of your product have remained high you have become aware that a foreign company intends to try to enter your home market.

What could you do to ensure that your sales are not too badly affected?

8. Utilising Production Capacity

You have recently invested heavily in new technology systems for your production line. Despite an advertising campaign, home sales have remained static and your new machinery is running at under-capacity.

What are the possible courses of action that you could take in order to use your machinery at a more economic rate?

9. Quality vs Mass-Production

Your company, which produces a high quality specialist product, is now being challenged by cheaper but lower quality products from the Far East. Until now your manu-facturing methods have used tradition-al crafts with none of the high technology, mass-production meth-ods introduced by your competi-tors.

What possible responses could be made to halt the slide in sales and which would be your preferred choice?

10. Fighting Off the Multinationals

Three years ago you created a company to sell cosmetic products made by outside manufacturers to your own natural recipe. Although you now have a chain of 5 shops, nationwide demand is out-stripping your ability to finance the opening of new shops and large multi-national cosmetic companies are beginning to notice your success.

What can you do to prevent them, with their superior financing facilities, from squeezing you out of the market?

11. Motivating Employees

You have just been appointed to the board of an unprofitable company that has recently been privatised. You have been asked to put forward proposals to remotivate staff who have been demotivated by various rumours of redundancies and by press criticisms of standards of service and efficiency.

Where should your priorities lie and how would you tackle the problem?

12. Staff Loyalty

The junior and middle management levels of your company have been seriously affected by the lack of promotion prospects and they have become a soft target for head-hunters and competing companies.

What are you going to do to ensure that your company does not lose vital staff?

13. Incentives or Rewards?

The Board of Directors of your company have asked you to present proposals for a new incentive scheme for your salesmen.

Discuss and decide on the objectives of the scheme. Should it encourage better results in the future or reward the good results in the past?

Draw up proposals for the details of the scheme.

14. Increasing Productivity

You are the Production Director of your company and want to find an incentive scheme to increase the productivity of production workers. What proposals could you put forward for discussion with the unions?

15. Reducing Costs

You are the Operations Manager of the company running the public bus system in your city. Your results for the last 6 months show that you will be running at a loss and operating costs must be cut.

What possible actions could you take to achieve the necessary reductions?

16. Changing Over to Automation

What are the advantages and disadvantages of a totally automated production system?

17. Modernising the Company Image

You have been brought in to up-date the image and services of a well-established but rather old-fashioned company.

Do you try to match the services and products offered by your competitors? What else could you do?

18. Staffing Problems

You work in the Personnel Department of a large supermarket chain. Many of your employees, mainly the check-out operators and shelf-stackers are young people under 20, who work part-time in the evenings and on Saturdays for comparatively low wages. With the birth-rate falling the supply of potential employees is declining.

What should you do?

19. Handling a Merger

Your company is considering merging with another who you frequently work with on large export projects. You work in similar but complementary rather than competitive areas of business and the merger would, therefore, not create redundancies.
What do you tell your staff about the discussions and when?

20. Flexi-Time

In what situations is flexi-time a workable proposal?
What are the disadvantages and advantages for various groups of workers?
What are the disadvantages and advantages for the company?

21. Managerial Qualities

What personal qualities are needed by a manager – not including professional knowledge or expertise.
Make a list of 10 qualities. Work in pairs.
Combine your list with the lists from other students and then rank them in order of importance.

22. A Suggestion Box?

What are the advantages and disadvantages of a suggestion scheme? (a scheme where employees suggest how the company's operations can be improved or money saved)
How should the suggestions be judged?
How should the suggestors be rewarded?

23. Language Policy

Your company has been taken over by an American company who have said that the company language is to be English and that all employees who have contact with the parent company have to be able to speak English.
Make a list of the types of employees who will need English and the types of courses which they could take.
Match the employees to the most appropriate course and explain how you will motivate them to learn quickly.

24. Student Sponsorship

Your company wants to set up a sponsorship scheme for students while they are at university.
What are the benefits of a scheme like this for the company and the students?
What provisions need to be made with regard to holiday work, payment for holiday work, payment while studying, obligations for both sides after the university course is finished?
What other points need to be considered?

Section 3   Business Ethics

1. Exploiting Cheap Labour

On a business trip to a Third World country you see an interesting and unusual product which you are sure could be successfully marketed in your own country at a price which would be both attractive to the consumer and profitable to you. When you visit the factory which makes this product you find that the working conditions of the workforce are bad and the pay rates low. Should you make a contract with them?

---

2. Lowering Your Standards?

You are the architect on a big prestigious project which unfortunately seems to be running into trouble over building costs. You know that the job has been over-engineered.
When someone offers you materials which are slightly below specification, what do you do? It could make the difference between the scheme being built or not.

---

3. Bribery

You are a law officer investigating a case of bribery. During your investigation you find that a few years ago one of the suspects was very friendly with your son. Your son has recently set up his own business and it is developing well. You are told that if the suspect is put on trial, either by you or anyone else, then your son's business will be ruined and he will never be able to have his own business again.
What could you do and what would you decide to do?

---

4. Sweeteners?

Your business has been going through a bad period but recently you have been negotiating for a long-term and valuable contract. At the last meeting you were taken on one side and told that the contract would be signed if you were prepared to make a payment into a numbered Swiss bank account operated by the chief negotiator on the other side.
What do you do?

5. Indirect Pressure

You are an independent insurance assessor and agent and your business has not been doing well recently. You are called in to investigate the damage after a factory fire and you are not convinced that the fire was accidental. The factory owner has been talking to you about recommending a friend to take out a lucrative new policy through you.
Do you say anything?
What would be the possible consequences both of speaking and of keeping quiet?

----

6. Going Back on Your Word

Two months ago your company took over a competitor who had a few months earlier re-equipped its factory with up-to-date machinery. At the time of the takeover you gave assurances to the workforce that there would be no job losses. Since the takeover you have tried unsuccessfully to raise finance for similar new machines in your original factory where you have a militant trade union. The easiest solution to the problem is to lay off the workforce in the recently acquired factory and transfer the machines to your own factory.
What problems would you face if you did this?
What action would be best and why?

----

7. Industrial Espionage

A competitor of yours has made a valuable technical breakthrough which will improve the quality of his product, reduce the cost of his production and will make *your* product uncompetitive. Someone approaches you offering to sell you details of the research which your competitor has done and which led to the breakthrough.
What do you do?

----

8. A Conflict of Interests

For a long time you have campaigned for a new airport in your area. The authorities have now agreed that it is necessary and want to build it in such a location that the flight path will pass over the village where you live. You live in an old, historic house in the village which has been owned by your family for several generations. Your family are settled in the area: your wife has her own business and your children are happy and successful in local schools.
What do you do?

9. A Vested Interest

You have been playing an active part in the opposition to a big civil engineering project in your area. You have been unofficially approached and told that a subsidiary of one of the companies involved in the project would be prepared to give your company a lucrative contract.
What should you do?

----

10. Kind or Corrupt?

As part of the assets of a merger your company has recently acquired a villa in Spain. You have an important contract with the local government coming up for renewal and you hear that the wife of their chief negotiator is ill and needs to spend the winter in a warm dry climate. Do you offer him the use of your empty villa in Spain?

----

11. Keeping Quiet about Pollution

The production process used in your factory is known, by your scientists, to produce pollution. At the moment it is not scientifically possible to test and prove this and so there is no legal obligation to change your process. There is an alternative process but it would make your product more expensive and therefore less competitive. What should you do?

----

12. Illegal Trade

You deal legally in curios made from animal skins etc. A potentially profitable new range is offered to you by your supplier but, although he says that the animals have not been illegally killed, there is still some doubt in your mind. What action should you take?

13. To Buy or not to Buy

The local government have decided to sell off a major part of the playing fields belonging to the local school and it has been re-zoned for business development and put on the market at a reasonable price. There has been an active local movement against the development. Your company, which supplies local shops, needs to have more warehouse space and your present warehouse is next to the playing-fields. What are the advantages and disadvantages of buying the land and what should you decide to do?

----

14. An Exclusive Agreement

You are a successful pop-star. A banking organisation offers to make a large payment to you, providing you agree that all tickets for your next world tour should be paid for using only their credit card.
What could be the good points and bad points of signing the contract?
What action(s) should you take?

----

15. Tobacco Sponsorship

You are a sportsman in need of sponsorship in order to train to compete in the next Olympic Games. You have been trying for a long time to find a sponsor and the only offer you have had is from a cigarette manufacturer. If you accept, you will have to wear their logo on all your sports equipment.
What are the pros and cons of accepting or rejecting their offer?
What would you do?

----

16. Withdrawing Your Product

The peak sales time for your company's product is always in the 3 months before Christmas. In October you find that there is a minor fault in the product. It is not dangerous but shortens the normal life of the product.
What could be the consequences of withdrawing it at this time and losing your sales?
Would you recommend withdrawing it immediately?

17. Profits vs the Environment

Your R & D department tells you that it would be possible for your production process to be changed so that it would not damage the environment. However, it would raise your product price, making it more expensive than the competition.
What possible actions could you take?
What would be the advantages, disadvantages and consequences of these actions?

---

18. Negotiate or Pay?

A foreign government has taken hostage your company's employees who are working in their country.
Do you either negotiate or pay a ransom for their release? What might be the consequences of taking either of these actions?
What else could you do?

---

19. Counterfeit Products

A supplier based in a foreign country offers you goods with a well-known and prestigious logo on them at a surprisingly low price. At that price you suspect that they must be copies but they would certainly deceive the customer.
Do you buy them and market them?
Is there anything else you would do?

---

20. A Question of Conscience

You have been negotiating to buy a property from the widow of a businessman whose firm went bankrupt. The stress of the failure gave him a heart attack and he left her with nothing but the property that you have been trying to buy. You hear from a friend that, in a few months, the land will be re-zoned by the local government and the value will increase dramatically.
What do you do: conclude the sale or tell the vendor?

21.   Owning up?

A colleague comes to you and tells you that after he left you in the pub last night he drove home. He does not remember that anything happened on the drive home but he heard that on the road which he used, someone was knocked down and is in hospital in intensive care. He noticed that there is a mark on his car which he does not remember seeing before.
What advice would you give to your colleague?
Would you do anything?

---

22.   Selling up and Selling out

You are part of a group of small traders fighting to keep a large and threateningly strong competitor out of your area. The company contacts you informally and offers to buy you out at a very favourable price.
What would be the pros and cons of accepting the offer and the pros and cons of refusing the offer?
What actions(s) would you take?

---

23.   Economising

You work in a company operating a bus system in your city and have asked your managers to suggest ways of cutting costs.
The 3 feasible schemes were either:
    a) redundancies
    b) wage cuts
    c) economies in the maintenance programme
What are the problems associated with agreeing to each of these options?
Which would you choose?

---

24.   Holding Prices Down

Inflation is high and many companies in your field feel that they are pricing themselves out of the market and have persuaded their employees to accept wage cuts. By this method the employees hope to hold down prices and maintain sales rather than face the possibility of short time or being laid off.
At the moment, sales of *your* product have not been affected.
Do you follow the lead of your competitors and negotiate pay cuts or leave things as they are?
What could be the positive and negative results of these two possible decisions?

25. Third World Dilemma

2 years ago your company, which produces food products invested in new machinery. For health reasons, the product which was made on this machinery is now banned in your own country. It is not yet banned in 3rd World countries.

Do you continue manufacturing this product and export it or do you write off this machinery?

What might be the consequences of choosing either of these possibilities?

---

26. A Risky Appointment

There is a vacancy for the most senior executive in one of your company's overseas subsidiaries. Both on paper and after interview the best candidate would seem to be a 35-year old woman with 2 children whose husband is a writer. She is a dynamic, ambitious and valuable member of your staff and she has made it known that she would probably leave the company if she is not given this promotion.

On the other hand, as a woman, she might not be well received by the country that she would be working in. This might affect the volume of business done by your company.

What do you do?

---

27. Disrupting Family Life

Recently your younger, male, married employees have become more and more reluctant to accept postings either within your own country or abroad. It has emerged that this is due to the fact that their wives are working and moving might mean the interruption of a promising career. Since it was made clear when they joined the company that postings have to be accepted except in exceptional circumstances, do you insist on employees moving or resigning, or do you find some other solution to this problem?

If so, what?

---

28. Looking to the Long-term?

Your company, a leader in the construction industry uses hardwood which is imported from a developing country as a disposable ingredient of the building process.

You know that:
1) the forests which are cut down are not replanted and that ultimately you will have to look elsewhere for your supply
2) the long term impact on the environment and people of the exporting country is detrimental despite the short term economic advantage that they are experiencing.

What do you do?

Teachers' **N**otes

The teachers' notes are divided into sections:

1. General notes
2. General workscheme for Business Problems
3. General workscheme for Business Issues and Business Ethics
4. Notes specific to individual units

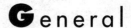
Always explain the activity fully and in your own words before giving the students any handout(s).

When moving from one stage of an activity to another, ensure that the students know exactly what their objective is in that particular stage of the activity.

General Objectives

The objective of these activities is to promote free discussion. Because in most situations in life it is important to arrive at a decision as quickly as possible, it may be necessary to remind the students that, in the situation of practising their English, it is the discussion that is important and that the decision is only of secondary importance.

The activities are intended to cover a variety of topics so that a wide variety of vocabulary can be practised. Prior to each activity an input session of relevant vocabulary can prove valuable.

Practice of Specific Language

These activities are designed primarily to promote fluency and confidence in discussion. If the teacher wishes to encourage the use of certain functions or structures this can also be done. Suggestions for language which can be practised in a natural way during the discussion are made for each unit.

Timing of Discussions

The length of the discussions will vary depending on the students involved. When a group is new to free discussions it can be valuable to specify a minimum period for discussion, reminding students that disagreement prolongs discussion. Remember that the motivation behind short discussions is usually a subconscious desire to achieve a decision as quickly as possible. Remind the students that a decision is not their primary objective here.

As far as specifying a maximum is concerned, it is usually easy to bring discussion to a close should this be necessary.

Encourage any groups that finish too quickly to continue their discussion – find out what they have decided and, where necessary, subtly input further ideas or alternatively, get them to plan their final presentations. Remind them that each member of the group will have to speak.

Choice of Group Structure

Other than where pairs are recommended, the optimum working group is usually 3 or 4 – this enables a good mixture of 'imaginative' (not to be confused with 'talkative') and 'non-imaginative' students. It is unwise to create a group with a mixture of quiet students and more voluble students. This usually deters the quiet students from contributing. A group of quiet students may need more encouragement during the discussion but they will eventually respond to the opportunity to talk.

If the group is a low level one and small in number, it is often valuable for the teacher to lead the first discussion asking each student for ideas and opinions. It enables students to get into the habit of taking part in a discussion in English.

Presentation of Findings

A short final presentation from each group of the decisions that they made and the reasoning behind them is useful both for fluency practice in a different environment and the possible use of the language of presentations. Allow other groups to question the presenting group and challenge them to justify their decisions.

Monitoring and Feedback

Discussions should be constantly monitored. Where there is mother-tongue interference, immediate, but selective, correction of mistakes can be helpful. Remember that too much immediate correction can inhibit fluency.

During the discussion input any vocabulary needed.

Feedback can be done in several ways:
  (i)   Write mistakes on an OHP slide – this can be photocopied later if required.
  (ii)   Write on paper what was said, hand out copies and get the students to correct it themselves. Give supervision.
  (iii) Write on paper what was said, correct it in a different colour, then hand it out for the students to study later.

notes *2*   **B**usiness **P**roblems

General Workscheme

Any recommended changes to the general workscheme can be found in the notes specific to individual units.

Stage 1

Give the students a general outline of the task in your own words.

Stage 2

Read the handout with the students and solve any vocabulary problems.

Stage 3

Divide the class into small groups.
(3 is probably the optimum number)

Stage 4

Optional – advisable to omit for lower levels
Remind the students of any specific language that they should be practising.

Stage 5

Student discussion with discrete monitoring from the teacher.

Stage 6

Each group presents their findings.
(Ensure that each student contributes)

Stage 7

Feedback session

(Ideas on possible VARIATIONS of these activities can be found in the notes specific to individual units.)

notes 3   Issues and Ethics

General Workscheme

Stage 1

Read the discussion topic with the students and solve any vocabulary problems.

Stage 2

In pairs students should draw up a list of possibilities with the pros and cons of each possibility.

Stage 3

Re-combine in groups of 3 or 4
(dividing the pairs from Stage 2).
Explain that each group may make up any specific details that they may need. However, they should not significantly change the problem.

Stage 4

Discuss and decide on a preferred course of action.
(teacher monitors)

Stage 5

Each group presents their findings.
(Ensure that each student contributes)

Stage 6

Feedback session

Alternative

You may wish to copy one page of topics, cut them up, and allocate a different topic to each student, pair, or group. You could lay them out and allow the students to choose, either selecting a favourite or randomly, "out of the hat". Students could then proceed in groups, exchange topics, and report.

notes 4   Individual Units

Unit 1   The Citibus Problem

Having completed Stages 1 - 4 remind the students that, as in real life, the budget available to them is not unlimited – don't let them simply throw money at the problems.

Possible Language

Do you have any ideas on what we ought to do about .....?
What do you recommend in order to solve the problem of .....?

Maybe we should/shouldn't .....
Perhaps we ought to .....
It might be a good idea to try .....
Have you thought of .....?
It seems to me that we should .....
We recommend .....

What a good idea.
That's a good suggestion.
That'd be worth trying.

Variation

Use both Units 1 and 2 and, when groups are constituted, allow the students to decide whether they wish to join the committee discussing buses or the one discussing trains. Try to ensure that the number of groups are as nearly equal as possible. The final presentation can then take the form of a joint bus/train users' committee.

Unit 2   The Cititrain Survey

see Unit 1

Unit 3   Company Cars

In stage 2 read only the first handout with the students.
After stage 3 the students should fill in the worksheet before being given the 'car information sheet' and repeating stage 2 with that.
Then continue with stage 4 etc.

Possible Language

––––––––er than / more –––––– than
the most –––––––– / the –––––––est

not / almost as ----- as
the same as -----
not ----- enough / too ------
Why don't we..... ?
What | about .....?
How |
X looks suitable for .....
Would X be a good idea for .....?

Unit 4   The Best Policy

Follow the general workscheme for Business Problems.

Possible Language

From the information we have, it seems to me that .....
I would be inclined to choose .....
Policy X | looks the best available
              | seems to cover everything we need
I would go for .....
My choice would be .....
Policy X is obviously not | what we need
                           | suitable for us

Variation

Introduce an information gap exercise before stage 4 by modifying the
handout and giving students incomplete information. This can be done by
blanking out information randomly or by making students responsible for 1 or
2 policies and asking them to obtain information about the other policies from
other students. They should have to obtain full information before moving on
to stage 5.

Unit 5   Moving House

For deviations from general workscheme see Unit 3.

Possible Language

It's got to be .....
It must be .....
What they want is .....
Ideally, it needs to be .....
They can't do without .....

It's | essential | that .....
      | important |
      | vital |
I think they'd like to have .....

Unit 6   A Staff Canteen

For deviations from general workscheme see Unit 3.
After preparing the company profile, the information on canteens and the
luncheon voucher scheme should be studied before moving on to stage 4.
Note that students have to decide whether to create a staff canteen or
provide luncheon vouchers. Preparation 1 is about the running of a canteen
and is intended to raise issues which will be relevant to the creation of a new
canteen.

Possible Language

As the company ...., we can't introduce scheme X
The company is ...., | therefore | we should ....
                          | for that reason |
                          | that's why |
System X would be successful because ....
System Y is impractical since ....
The system is difficult to organise, that's why it wouldn't work for us
We need system X in order to ....
We would prefer to have system Y so that ......

Variation

An information gap exercise could be included by dividing the students into 2
groups, one with information about canteens and the other with information
about luncheon vouchers. They should be encouraged to summarise their
information before talking to a student from the other group.

Unit 7   Relocating the Factory

Follow the general workscheme for Business Problems.

Possible Language

We have to X before we can Y
We can't X before we Y
We really shouldn't X until we have Y-ed
We could X and then we could Y
X-ing must come after Y-ing
First we must X
Next we should Y
Oughtn't we to X later
As soon as | we've
When |
We could X

72

Possible Solution

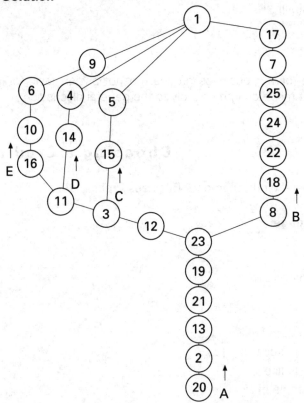

Unit 8   Business Travellers

After stage 2 allow pairs to decide which services could be introduced immediately and which need time to introduce.

In stage 3 assign the pairs a particular task: Finance, Marketing or Personnel and get them to discuss the impact on their particular department and fill in the appropriate part of the worksheet. Before stage 4 re-assign the students to groups of 3 – ensure that you have at least one Finance, one Marketing, and one Personnel Mananger in each group.

Possible Language

More businessmen would travel if we introduced ....
Business passengers will increase if we introduce......
Passengers will decrease unless ......
Traffic will increase providing we ....
The number of passengers will rise as long as we ......
I agree / That's right
I couldn't agree more
Given the situation I can see that ....

You may be right / I'm not sure (about that)
I don't agree (at all).

Variation

For lower level or non-business groups, do not assign tasks or fill in the worksheets but move on immediately to the general discussion.

Unit 9   Choosing a Credit Card

Follow the general workscheme for Business Problems.

Possible Language

Although ......
..........., however ....
In spite of ....
Despite ....
Even though ....
X has features | such as | ....
               | like |
X is a good example of ......
For example | , with X ....
For instance |

Variation

1. Insert an information gap exercise by dividing the students into 3 groups and giving each group information about a different card. The students should obtain complete information before discussing.

2. Students decide which card is the best in a general situation.

Unit 10   Working Conditions

Follow the general workscheme for Business Problems. Insert pair work during Stage 2 to prepare a list of the work done by the Office Services Department before reading the complaints. Distribute the roles equally and when each group has read their roles and decided on their preferred solutions, bring the 2 groups together, in pairs, to roleplay a meeting.

Emphasise the necessity of keeping information secret.

Possible Language

We | could | ask for ......
    | might |
They may consider doing X to improve things .....
We can offer ......
We would be willing to .....
What would you say if we ....?
Our proposal would be to .....
We could accept this only if .....

Variation

1. If numbers demand, introduce other roles: eg Department heads
2. Roleplay the meeting in larger groups.

Unit 11   Business Entertaining

Follow the general workscheme for Business Problems and any notes on the handouts.

Possible Language

Our clients would enjoy .....
We would be able to .....
We would transport them by .....
X would be appreciated .....
As a result of ......
..... and therefore .....
.... hence .....
As a consequence of .....

Unit 12   Joining the Team

Study the initial information with all the students together before dividing them into 2 groups and giving each group information about only one of the athletes. Organise an information exchange. Stages 5, 6 and 7 should follow.

Possible Language

Where was X born?
How | old | is she?
     | fit |
What medals has she won?
What major events has she competed in?
How did she perform in ...?

Instead of .....
.... could ..... instead.
As an alternative ......
Either ...... or .....

Unit 13   Famine Aid Album

Having explained the task, divide the students into 2 groups and give each
group information about a different band. Then get them to read the
information carefully and pick out the important points putting them under
headings such as, details of band members, past chart success, involvement
in charity, live appearances, fan response, tours etc.
In pairs, one from each group, exchange information and when they both
have complete information, ask them to decide which band will be asked to
record the last track for the album.

Stages 6 and 7 of the workscheme should follow.

Possible Language

Is the band .... ?
Did the band ..... ?
What have the band ..... ?
Have the band ever ..... ?
When did the band record ..... ?
Who plays in the band?
How popular is the band?
Instead of .....
.... could ..... instead.
As an alternative ......
Either ...... or .....

Unit 14   Employee Development

Follow the general workscheme for Business Problems.

Possible Language

Course X will benefit ......
Course X will help .....
Y will find it easier to .....
Choosing a team will .....
The team will work more efficiently ......
Y will use his time .....
It's certain that a course on ....
It's quite likely that .....

It's highly unlikely that an improvement .....
I doubt if X will benefit .....
It's not out of the question that ......

Variation

The information about the courses could be distributed in such a way that it was possible to include an information gap element in the activity.

Unit 15   Selling Instanews

For workscheme see unit 12.

Possible Language

Don't forget how good .....
You must admit that X would be a convenient .....
Have you considered the impact of .....
As you know we provide .....
I think that I have already said that the facility.....
Did I mention the service which ..... ?
Etc.

Unit 16   Appointment Board

Follow the notes given on the handouts. The final discussion should take the form of a role play.
The following roles are essential:
    Daniel Archer – Founder and former MD of Archer Electronics
    Ann Archer – Wife of Daniel Archer, mother of Claude Fund
    Jean Brett – daughter of Daniel Archer, wife of Michael Brett
    Michael Brett – Managing Director
    Geoff Butcher – Production Director

Other roles could be added: Personnel Manager, Marketing Manager, etc.

Possible Language

In actual fact, X is well qualified ......
In point of fact, he contributed well to .....
On the contrary he is a positive influence .....
Actually, he refused our offer to .....
Sorry to | interrupt | but, ...
           | butt in |
Could I say something here .....?

If I may come in here .....
If you would allow me to continue .....
Just a moment.
If I might finish .....

Unit 17   Strengths and Weaknesses

Distribute the general information sheet, and, in pairs, get the students to draw up the organigram described in the handout. Then give out the different information sheets in approximately equal numbers of A,B and C. Then follow the notes given on the handouts.

Possible Language

There are X departments
There is a Y department with a Z section
The X Manager is responsible to the Y Manager
The X Manager is responsible for Z clerks
The X Manager needs to be .....
A Virgo is good at .....
A Scorpio hasn't got the right temperament for ....
A Pisces is too ..... / not ...... enough.
A Libra would cause problems as a ....

Unit 18   Trade Fair Venue

Follow the notes given on the handouts.

Possible Language

Although ......
......, however .....
In spite of / Despite .....
Even though .....
I think .....
In my opinion .....
What do you think about .....
Are you in favour of / against ..... ?

Variation

Omit the information gap element by giving all the students all the data.

When the students have read the information sheet, divide them into groups of 3 and give them one of the worksheets – half the groups should prepare a presentation on the 'design and planning' part of the project and the other half should prepare a presentation on the 'operations' part of the project.

Encourage them to produce visuals which illustrate the basic facts on which they should elaborate, when they speak. It is advisable to provide them with flip chart paper, OHP slides and pens etc.

Possible Language

The aim of this presentation is to .....
I'd like to begin by .....
First of all ...., secondly ...., next ...., finally ....
Turning to .....
That brings me to .....
In addition .....
Not only .... but also .....
Let me give an example .....
Although ....., we have to remember .....
The main advantage of ..... is that .....
Looking at this illustration, it is quite clear that .....
As you can see from the diagram .....
A very interesting point is that .....
In conclusion, I'd like to say .....

Other Business Titles from LTP

Basic Telephone Training
Anne Watson Delestrée

A unique package of book plus cassette. A highly practical and immediately useful course making elementary students proficient in this speicalised area.
Book 0 906717 42 6   Cassette 0 906717 47 7

Build Your Business Vocabulary
John Flower

A very user-friendly book of graded exercises practising a comprehensive range of business vocabulary.
0 906717 87 6

The Language of Meetings
Malcolm Goodale

A course for all students who have to participate in meetings in English at in-company or international level. Very practical exercise material.
0 906717 46 9

Business Partners
Pearson Brown and John Allison

A lower intermediate course in business English – suited to the needs of elementary students who need to use English at work.
Students' Book 0 906717 81 7   Workbook 0 906717 82 5
Cassette   0 906717 83 3   Teachers' Book 0 906717 84 1

Business English
Peter Wilberg and Michael Lewis

Business English is unique course material embodying the principles of the negotiated syllabus, the centrality of student input, and the importance of vocabulary and collocation for ESP students. Highly commended in the English Speaking Union ELT Book Awards, Business English is published as a conventional book or in an A4 looseleaf file.

Bound Edition 0 906717 72 8   Teachers' Manual 0 906717 80 9
A4 Looseleaf Edition 0 906717 97 3

If you would like more information about LTP's Business English list, please write requesting our Catalogue to:

LTP
35 Church Rd
Hove BN3 2BE